Route 66 Races

"Competition is about inspiring each other
to apply our potential for the better of all."
                                    -Doug H. Knutson

The Events

In this sixth volume of the series, we will cover
the topic of events; build classes, races, seasons,
season points, leagues and championships.

Each of these topics may have their own volume
for more detailed coverage, however, for now, the
idea is to introduce these concepts for preliminary
awareness.

The scope of variations that are able to be offered
to the community is much larger than we are able
to cover in this one volume, so consider this to be
a preface to following volumes on those topics.

preface

ROUTE 66 Races

The Build Classes

Several aspects of car building classes have been discussed in Volume 1 of this series.

Build Classes are essential for introducing fine motor skills to many who have not experienced the science, technology, engineering and math that is able to help them think better in life.

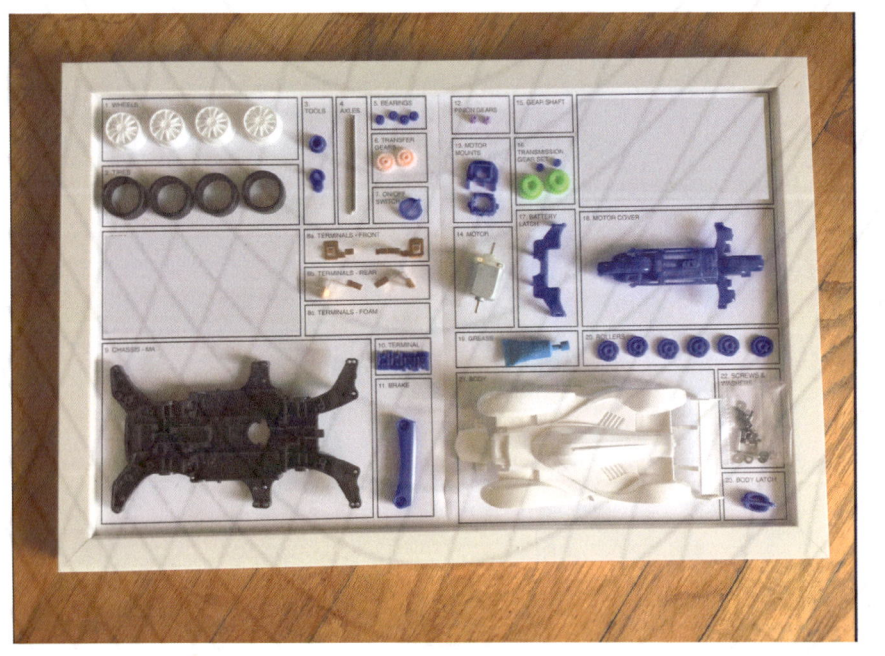

Build Class Parts Trays help keep parts in order and prevent loss.

to apply our potential for the better of all."
                                            -Doug H. Knutson

The Races

Several aspects of the race events have been covered in Volume 1 of this series.

Here, we will cover more about the marshals, drivers, teams, owners and sponsors with regards to the actual race events.

The Marshals

Marshals are expected to be unbiased even though every human has their hidden biases.

It might even be best to find marshals who are not interested in racing or do not know any of the racers.

Furthermore, a person with a perceived high moral character may be a better marshal than a person with more skill or talent for the job.

ROUTE 66 Races

The Marshals (continued)

The main task of a marshal is to assist in the passing of one car by another car.

The skill or talent here, is for the marshal to know all of the participating cars for in which speed class they are so that the marshal knows which car is about to pass which other car.

Too many times, a marshal, who does not know the cars, will mistakenly assist a slower car to pass a faster car only because the slower car temporarily appears to be catching up to the faster car.

The next task of a marshal is to call out to other marshals, if any, the warnings of yellow flag or red flag when their are incidents on the track that will impede other cars or if a car leaves the track.

3

to apply our potential for the better of all."
-Doug H. Knutson

ROUTE 66 Races

The Drivers

Drivers are the ones actually handling their car for pitstops and repairs during the race events.

For remote racing, the driver allows the track host to handle their car during the race with possibly limited pitstop and repair capability.

The driver's name is listed in the leaderboard for each race for fans and competitors to see.

The driver does not necessarily own the car that they are handling, especially if the driver is leasing the car from the track host or has a team or business sponsor who owns the car.

The Teams

A Team is a group of drivers and mechanics that are all using the same logo of a private or business sponsor.

Team drivers may own their own cars, yet the team is encouraged to share strategies and even share parts for repairs during race events.

A team may form a cooperative in order to buy a large number of parts for sharing at a lower wholesale price.

Teams must remain intact for an entire season in order to receive team points from all members toward the championship standings.

to apply our potential for the better of all."
-Doug H. Knutson

The Owners

Owners may own a single car or a own a team of cars and all of the parts needed for repairs.

A Driver may be an owner, yet is not allowed to race multiple cars since they are participating in the actual racing and may show bias.

Owners of teams may not participate in the actual racing and must remain the owner for an entire season in order to receive owner points toward the championship standings.

Owners are allowed to obtain sponsorships from sponsors which pay the owners for putting their sponsor logo and information on the team cars and other allowable surfaces.

ROUTE 66 Races

The Sponsors

Sponsors, whether private or business, are able to provide financial sponsorships to individual drivers, to teams, to owners of teams, to individual build classes, to individual race events including qualifying and the main race.

Sponsors may even sponsor individual seasons such as Spring, Summer, Autumn and Winter.

Sponsors may sponsor a section of a track or sponsor the whole entire track and any other approved surfaces around the track.

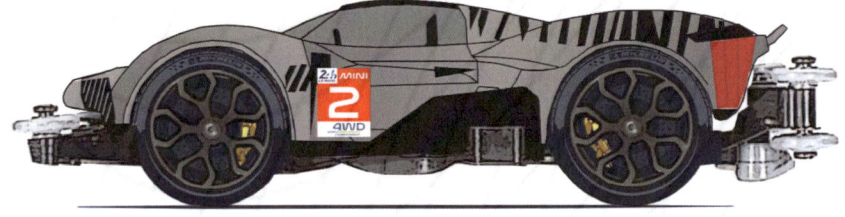

On the highest level, a sponsor may sponsor on the state or national level for individual state championships and/or for the entire 8-state league championship each year.

Online Event Attendance

Build classes and race events are able to be attended in person or online if available.

To attend a build class online, a track host would need to arrange class times manage that event, most likely, separate from an in-person build class.

To attend a race event online, a driver would need to arrange to lease a car and purchase a repair and maintenance package, allowing the track host or reliable other person to handle that driver's car during and between each race.

Otherwise, a driver would need to arrange the shipment of their own car to the track location and purchase a repair and maintenance package for the season and then arrange for the return shipment of their car if they want it back at the end of any season or end of year.

In-Person Events

Drivers attending race events in person should show respect for other drivers by showing up very early to each race event since the race is expected to start at a certain time and end at a certain time, allowing other drivers to leave the track at the expected time in order to attend to other important tasks in their life.

Depending on the number of drivers in a race and other factors, qualifying is better to be done on a previous day to the main race event.

Otherwise, if qualifying on the same day, there should be at least one hour between the end of qualifying and the start of the main race event in order to give drivers the time to prepare.

All drivers will be provided with identical pitstop amenities clear of any obstructions for quick access to and from the track.

The Driver - Marshal Relationship

Drivers prepare their cars and repair their cars yet, marshals are responsible for placing cars on the track and for removing cars from the track for passing or for mechanical failure or other track-blocking incidents.

A marshal will do their best to deliver a disabled car to the proper driver and the driver will not collect their car from the track or from off track should their car leave the track.

A driver will not place their car on the track or be anywhere near enough to the track for any careless action may result in any interference with the track or other drivers' cars.

The marshal's task is a difficult one and they may make a few mistakes which are able to be challenged by drivers to the race command, yet should not disrespect any marshal.

ROUTE
66
Races

The Qualifying

As with most qualifying events, the positional order for each class is determined by a qualifying session.

For these purposes, each car is allowed three (3) laps for registering their best lap time.

From the end of the qualifying session, each car will be impounded by the track host or by a marshal and no work may be done to the cars except for the removal of batteries which will be done under the watch of a marshal.

In the case of multiple classes, the classes will be qualifying for positions in their own class, not for being mixed into different classes even if a car qualifies with a faster or slower speed than a car in another speed class.

All cars must meet minimum or maximum speed class limits.

11

The Car Numbers

Each speed class has its own set of available car numbers.

At the beginning of a new year of racing, each driver will need to qualify in a position that merits the car number that they desire unless that driver finished in any of the top three (3) positions of their speed class in the previous year.

Any available car number may be auctioned off by the current driver or owner to another driver or owner, before or after a season.

If a driver desires to have a number that is already taken, that driver could demand an auction if that driver has qualified at a faster speed at the beginning of a new yearly season and only obtains that number if he is willing to pay more than the current driver is willing to pay.

12

The Seasons

Spring, Summer, Autumn and
Winter are the four seasons of the racing year.

Each season consists of 12 weekly races each,
resulting in 48 races per year with 4 weeks left
over for the state and national championships.

Qualifying takes 2 hours per week, so the total
hours per week of track time for the league
championships is about 4 hours.

This leaves a lot of extra time for build classes,
track maintenance, repair and maintenance of
equipment and cars of drivers who are racing
remotely.

There is plenty of time for more and other
types of racing during each week, like 4-hour
to 24-hour race lengths and specialty races with
single or multiple speed classes involved.

The Speed Classes

Drivers may enter and exit speed classes at any time during a season, yet will not be able to carry their former speed class points with them to their latter speed class.

Also, each speed class is limited to 8 cars with a recommendation of a 6-car limit per race.

A track host's limit should be respected.

The number of cars allowed to qualify for any race is only limited by the track host's time.

Therefore, any new driver may have a chance to qualify for a position in any new race before the qualifying time is up for the day.

New drivers are also able to offer to buy a place in the qualifying lineup if another driver is willing to swap places in line.

The Season Points

Points are awarded per race, per
speed class, for most laps led, for teams, for cars,
for owners and for the "spirit of the race".

The following amount of points are awarded:

1st position	25 points
2nd position	18 points
3rd position	15 points
4th position	12 points
5th position	10 points
6th position	8 points
7th position	6 points
8th position	4 points

Most laps led	2 points
SOTR award	2 points

Points for cars, teams and owners are based on
different parameters based on positions.

15

to apply our potential for the better of all."
-Doug H. Knutson

The State Leagues

Each state has its own league of competitors with season points accruing for state-specific awards.

State awards for drivers, cars, teams, owners and track hosts are provided for by state-wide sponsorships in exchange for marketing the sponsor to the state league audience base.

Drivers may cross state lines to participate in other leagues in person or remotely since a league track in their own state may not be located nearby.

In fact, any driver from anywhere in the world may join any race in any state as long as they are following the guidelines for joining.

Clearly though, drivers who arrive in person to races have a huge advantage for repairs and maintenance issues.

The National 8-State League

Concurrently, with each state league, the national league will run, consisting of all qualifying drivers in all eight (8) states.

National awards for drivers, cars, teams, owners track hosts and states, are provided for by nation-wide sponsorships in exchange for marketing sponsor to the league audience base.

Only drivers with top finishing positions in each state are allowed to participate in the final race event for national awards and recognition.

Any driver from anywhere in the world may qualify for participation in nationals as long as they follow the guidelines for qualifying.

Clearly, again, drivers who arrive in person to races have a huge advantage for repairs and maintenance issues.

The Championship

The road to the championship race starts at the local track.

Drivers sign up with the track host to join the local league and are automatically signed up for the state and national league for gathering season points.

The top three (3) drivers, from each speed class, at the local level from each local track along the route, are able to have their lap times compared with the lap times of every other top driver in their state, by speed class.

The positions of the state championship race are determined by those driver lap times.

The top three (3) position finishers, of each speed class, from the state championship races, or 168 drivers, will determine the national race participants.

The Championship Race

Those top three (3) drivers, from each speed class, at the state level from each state along the route, totaling 168 drivers, are able to have their lap times compared with the lap times of every other top driver in the nation, by speed class.

The available 66 positions of the national championship race are determined by those driver lap times, by class.

Since 66 cars divided by 7 speed classes results in nine (9) cars per class in the national race event, there will be three (3) spots left.

Those three (3) spots will be awarded to one of the next seven (7) fastest lap times, one per speed class, determined by the best nomination story submitted by their local track host, to be voted on by Route 66 Races race control team.

to apply our potential for the better of all."
-Doug H. Knutson

The Track Host

The track host is the person who may provide the property and/or the building of the track and/or manage the races.

It is not necessary for the track host to pay any fee to Route 66 Races to be part of the racing championship league.

All fees that the track host charges drivers are determined by the track host and are only possibly influenced by guideline suggestions by the Route 66 Races race control team based on adequate fairness.

The Route 66 Races company will earn the trust of track hosts by providing great support and by providing merchandise for marketing the local, state and national locations and events, thereby providing funding all of the free support to all local track hosts.

ROUTE 66 Races

The Race Reporters

Every great race is a great story to be watched and to be told or to be written down for others to read, later.

This is why Route 66 Races needs really great race reporters or journalists who are able to take video and/or write down all of the fun things that happened during each and every race.

These fun things include the weather, the temperature, the start time, any incidents that happen, like which drivers had pit stops, how long were the pit stops, and which cars had incidents and whether the car continued or if it was the end of the day for them.

Race reporters may be hired by track hosts or by Route 66 Races race control team to get the best detailed stories for sharing with the world and to get more people involved.

The Spectators

ROUTE
66
Races

On race days, there will most likely be a lot of spectators coming along with the drivers.

Only the track host, marshals and drivers are allowed within 20 feet of the track.

This allows for marshals to perform their task which will involve retrieving cars for handing off to the drivers who will be performing pitstops at least 10 feet away from the track.

Spectators are expected to show manners and be well-behaved including the responsibility of bringing their own trash bag like they are on a hiking trip-

     "carry out what you carried in."

Pet owners should be responsible enough to not bring pets to the track as the pet may interrupt a race.

ROUTE
66
Races

The Weather

Most tracks are going to be outside in the weather.

Therefore, many race days may be rained out or snowed out, leaving those drivers without additional season points toward the state and national championships.

Having some sort of track heating installed in the ground under the track may help melt ice and snow and dry the rain off of a track.

Covering the track may prove to be too much work, especially like using a tarp in high winds.

For those days where a race is canceled or in the instance of a red flag that ends a race before the official ending time, track hosts may use the position and points earned from the previous race as the official results for that race.

Finishing The Race

Although some races may be rained out or canceled, races ended by a red flag should be handled differently.

In a red flag ended race, at least 70% of the normal amount of laps will have needed to have been completed by the lead car in order for the entire field to receive any points.

Otherwise, if under 70%, the track host will use the same points earned from the previous race event.

During a full race, for a driver to receive any points, that driver must complete 70% of the laps completed by the lead car in its class.

If there are no other cars in its class, the 70% applies to the laps completed by the next lower speed class lead car's completed laps.

ROUTE
66
Races

The Post-Race Inspection

The only part of the car that needs
to be inspected after each race event is the
chassis.

Each chassis should be marked with a unique
mark by the track host before each race and a
photo should be taken of that mark.

At the end of each race or at the end of the race
for any particular car hoping to collect points,
will be impounded by a marshal until the chassis
inspection is finished.

After the entire race event is over, the track host
will confirm that no car exceeded its speed limit
for the speed class in which it raced.

Working transponders are the responsibility of
each driver, so if any laps are not registered by
the lap receiver, that lap is considered to be not
counted.

25

to apply our potential for the better of all."
-Doug H. Knutson

The Award Ceremony

After each race event, the track host may or may not offer an awards ceremony depending on time constraints of the day or due to the car inspection and lap speed inspection processes.

If the awards are awarded on race day or on another day, once the award is given, the data is not able to be changed.

It is important to get the data confirmed and registered with Route 66 Races race control before awarding any awards or trophies.

Trophies may or may not be awarded by the track host and yet, if trophies are awarded, the track host may offer their own type of award or trophy or has the option to purchase Route 66 Races trophies for each event.

Route 66 Races race control will provide trophies for state and nationals.

Route 66 Races is in association with
Route66Artists.com | Mini4WD.com | 66TheRoute.com
Route66Chess.com | Route66Savings.com |
Route66Organic.com
Route66Family.com | Route66Friends.com |
Route66Farms.com
Whoot66.com | Whoof66.com | 22Camels.com

MINI 4WD ENDURANCE
ROUTE
66
RACING
™

If you are interested in building and hosting
a "Route 66 Races" race track or
if you are an artist interested in contributing
your Route 66 related artwork or lyrics,
please send a text to 949-424-6496
or email donutbookscom@gmail.com.

1926-2026
Made In America